SOUL BIRD

Poems for Flying

Deborah Anne Quibell

MANDORLA BOOKS
WWW.MANDORLABOOKS.COM

Somewhere, deep within, you know. The soul bird has been
buried for too many tired years.

And she knows the way out.

And soon.

Her sweet call will swell from your pulse out into the world
that needs her so.

*This collection of poems is dedicated to my mother—the eyes
that see, the heart that holds, the love that believes, and the
force that has always beckoned forth
my greatest potential.*

CONTENTS

INTRODUCTION

I don't want to say much here.

Perhaps, because I long for the poems contained in this small volume to speak for themselves.

Poems, much like paintings and other works of art, are about *encounter*. They are as much about you as they are about me. They are as much yours as they are mine. We meet the poetry and in the process, we (often) meet something deep within ourselves. There is a stirring. An awakening. A response of some sort that leaves us altered or in touch with something rather mysterious and undeniably transformative.

The beauty and power of any artistic expression is that it often sparks and speaks to something universal in our human experience. I felt this with the mystics I read at an early age. "Surely, these poems are written for me," I would think over and over again in my heart. I was amazed at how much their words resonated in the most vulnerable, secret corners of my being.

I hope there is similar resonance for you as you make your way through these poems, all of which I have written, and yet offer to you not feeling as if they are mine at all.

But I do have a confession to make before we dive in.

Poetry, for me, is synonymous with vulnerability. Sharing this volume is like standing stripped before you, holding my naked, pounding, mystical heart in my bare hands. Offering it to you. Hoping you may find pieces of your own.

I began writing very early in my youth when a strong yearning for an intimate relationship with God gave rise to a collection of scribbled writings. The scribbled writings were my secrets—the conversations and longings that took up a fair amount of my time behind a locked bedroom door. Occasionally, I would share them shyly with my mother but very few others.

I suppose I worried of ridicule. Or, even worse, of being misunderstood.

God, to me, never felt like a single, fatherly entity in the sky. Perhaps, the concept began that way, but it didn't stick for very long. I grew up in the Catholic tradition, and would close my eyes a lot during mass on Sundays. Someone would usually nudge me thinking I was falling asleep, but I wasn't. I was simply trying to tune in to some mysterious, holy presence that seemed to pervade everything, and never felt far away.

It wasn't long before I stumbled upon the poetry and writing of the mystics, and fell in love. There was a casual intimacy with which they spoke to God, and with which God spoke to them. And when I read the exchange, I felt as if their words were slowly inscribed onto the walls of my heart. I wondered if they had been there as etchings all along—simply needing to be more deeply carved, noticed, and cared for.

And so I began writing poetry—around the age of five but much more seriously in my teens—because I couldn't *not*. It became my way of fostering a complex and often tumultuous relationship to some *Voice* within me. The V is capitalized here because it felt other-worldly and undeniably sacred.

In depth psychology, we talk about the Self—the numinous ordering principle within the psyche. In some Eastern traditions, this is known as the *Atman* or god within. The terminology mattered less to me. I just knew that I had to cultivate a relationship to the holy part of my being and the holy aspects of my existence. Call them what you may.

To this day, I don't quite understand the mechanism of my poetic expression. And I don't think I am meant to. The same way we never truly understand what happens or where we go during deep meditative practices. The experience (and its residue) is what matters.

Sometimes, I feel as if the Voice is rising up from a deep place within me—swirling upward from the depths. Sometimes, I feel as if the top of my head cracks open and the Voice comes down—descending from above. The movement seems to flow in both directions. Reaching up and descending down—my poetry straddling the gap somewhere between divinity and humanity, between the sacred and the profane, honoring both sides, both Voices. You will find this is mirrored in the shifting perspective of the poems contained in this volume. Sometimes, the Voice speaks to me. Sometimes, I speak to the Voice. A lot of times, I am not sure who is speaking.

As you read the poems in this collection, you may feel as if I am talking to you. In some ways, our hearts are most definitely conversing. But these pieces are as much reminders for me, as for you, dear friend and fellow seeker.

Maybe you have had similar encounters with a wise Voice within you? Perhaps, it comes as your conscience. Perhaps, it visits as bursts of creative inspiration. Perhaps, it appears when you pray or become very quiet in meditation. Perhaps, it awakens in nature. For me, it comes in a myriad of ways, but has found a clear path through poetry.

Writing poetry transports me to an experience far away from our daily existence, and yet remains intimately connected to it. It is not hard to tell when I have been writing. Just look for a hazy, distant look in my eyes and a deep sense of introverted silence. It usually takes me a while to return to Earth.

It has taken me many years to allow my behind-closed-door poems (my mystical secrets) to make their way out into the world. So tread, gently, if you don't mind. Even though I have always written prolifically, I kept my poems close, guarded them as my most treasured secrets.

But slowly, as I started to allow them to seep out into the world, I found them taking on a whole new life outside of myself. It was as if the poems were given wings, and the words allowed others to fly to the same sacred and holy places within themselves.

This collection is called *Soul Bird* because the poems that it holds on its pages are the true songs of the soul, as it learns to trust, escape, love, suffer, and grow. As it learns to be exposed and vulnerable and courageous and expressive. As it learns to break out of conformity, insecurity, and unworthiness, and fly into a heart-centered, unique, and mystical way of living.

Hopefully the poems will fly into your heart, inspiring your unique expression and flight, as well, beautiful friend.

Let us begin.

The cage door is never locked.

And if we stay inside, our heart will never know the freedom of flying.

"Run my dear, from anything that may not strengthen your precious budding wings. Run like hell my dear, from anyone likely to put a sharp knife into the sacred, tender vision of your beautiful heart."

~Hafiz

Soul Bird

Poems for Flying

BEAUTY IN REVELATION

You don't have to know any secrets.

The beauty of the poppy is the poppy.
The magnificence of the bee is the bee.
The radiance of the oak is the oak.

Don't search for anything
that is not immediately presented to you.

Be with things as they are
and they will reveal themselves further.

Don't get caught in your pilgrimage
and forget how to gasp.

Beauty has left
our constructed concepts
and is simply waiting
to be found
in the holy particularity
of things.

SCARLET-CHESTED SUNBIRD

Magnificent being,
come out from behind yourself.

The old, tired stories
that strangle and keep you small
must be re-told
into mythic tales
of stalks
and scarlet-chested sunbirds.

And as you emerge
from beneath the parched, holy ground
be warned
who you were before
will not recognize
the stranger you are becoming

You will no longer
yearn to fly
so close to the sun,
but will inhabit,
perhaps for the first time,
your marvelous,
Earthly body
of belonging.

THE SOIL OF YOUR INNER LIFE

Be selective.
With your time. Your energy.
And who you let in
to the doorway of your heart.

The soft soil of your inner life
is not a stomping ground.

Not a place for the curious taker or thief.
Not a place for the envious or judgmental.
Or anyone who wants to keep you small.

It is a place only for those
who breathe in
your radiance, vulnerability and brokenness
with a hushed awe and reverence.
Who bow before the glowing scars
and silvered shards of pain.

It is a place only for those
who intimately understand
(and deeply honor)
the (whole) divinity
you are working to reveal.

LET SILENCE NESTLE IN

Find a calm corner in your heart.

Take the voices of others
and ask them (politely) to wait outside.

Close the door.
Peel the whispers from the walls
and stack them neatly away.

Sweep aside the dust
(and lovingly smash the clock).

Invite the soft grass from the fields
and call, quietly, upon the wind.

When she arrives, smile
and gently blow your confusion,
your frustration, and your ache
to her care.

Lay down.

Relax.

Let silence nestle in.

This is your space
undisturbed and sacred.

After some time here,
the stars will appear

to show you the coordinates
of your next destination.

You don't have to know the map.

CUT THE STRINGS THAT KEEP YOU SMALL

There is no one who can define you.

Wild, beautiful soul,
you were not crafted for puppetry.

(So cut the strings that keep you small).

Stop asking for permission.

Don't search for your own beauty
Inside of someone else.

(You heart is wise and resplendent).

Don't believe the old, foolish stories.

(You don't need to please anyone).

Don't stay put on the shelf
of someone else's dream.

(Get down!)

Remember.

Power does not come from deceiving anyone.

(Not even yourself).

Your true powers are only given,
when you lay your weapons down,

when your kindness is uncompromising,
and when you don't, for a single second,
imagine a life lived for anything less than love.

Then

(and only then)

can you truly be called a creator.

Then

(and only then)

can you converse with the skies

to plot
your own destiny.

SOUL BIRD

There will come a time,
when you will be asked
to place your inner belongings
at the feet of a Love you are yet to know.

That to which your heart clings the most
will be asked of you.

You may be angry at the request.

You may scream and weep
until your tears can no longer
extinguish the flames
that burn the hands of your heart.

You may feel betrayed at the demand.

You may resist and fight
until your strength can no longer
hold back the shovel
that is digging up your soul.

Lay down, sweet one.
Let the clearing happen.

Somewhere, deep within, you know.

The soul bird
has been buried
for too many tired years.

And she knows the way out.

And soon.

Her sweet call will swell
from your pulse
out into the world
that needs her so.

A SPIRITUAL PROMISE

I will continue
to purify
and improve myself.

I will make
a conscious effort
to transform,
to become more conductive,
and less resistant.

I will practice.
and study.
I will give generously.

But, I will also know
and trust
the revelation of divinity
that has begun
in my heart
and in my being.

For every longing to be better,
I will breathe in the recognition
that I am enough,

For every word of critique,
I will add two words of love.

LATE ARRIVAL

Just for a moment
Stop with the should's
and should not's.

And entertain the hypothesis
that wherever you are
is good enough.

Don't let the constant clamor of tasks
become your symphony.

The orchestra of the heart
is performing
to an empty theater.

Listen to the whistle
of your imagination.

He has been waiting, patiently,
with his top hat and white gloves
to usher you in.

Leave your critical head in the car.

Tip-toe quietly
to your seat,
and shake hands with your dreams.

Don't make excuses.

Just smile and apologize that you are late.

YOUR BAREFOOT FRIEND

The holy waits for you,
like a friend without shoes.

You don't have to wash your feet 108 times
or sprinkle your toes with golden dust
before walking through the door.

You don't have to bathe in holy water
or adorn yourself with perfection
in order to sit down and enter.

You don't have to kneel, repent
Or say a thousand rosaries
To be granted access and grace.

You don't have to scrub your tired hands
or drape yourself in realization
prior to coming in.

Come in, as you are, my friend
weary, bloody, and broken,
without shoes.

Here you will find the golden dust at your feet,
the inner, holy waters in which you must bathe
grace like rain upon you
and the seed of divine perfection.

Here, in the mystery of the world,
you will find your way of being in it.

Here your Friend awaits,
barefoot and smiling
wondering what took you so long.

YOU DO NOT HAVE TO BE ENLIGHTENED

Be tender when there is an ache inside of you.

As tender as the soft ocean
that washes over you at dawn.

Your false notions
of 'strength'
will dissolve
under your magnificent ability
to allow.

They have no place here,
among the sacred cellar
of the heart's labor.

Your rawness is what is real.

Let it be what it is.

You do not have to be anywhere
or anyone
you are not.

You do not have to have it all figured out.

You do not have to pull it together.

You do not have to be enlightened.

What you truly feel
is what you must place

16

on the altar.

What you truly feel
is what will bring you
to your honest place
of worship.

WAKE UP CALL

Every once in a while. . .

Wake up before the sun.

Tip-toe softly into the silence.

Welcome the dark beauty of mystery.

Close your eyes
and sit
without an agenda.

Allow the gentle miracle
of your own existence
to whisper your heart awake.

Let your mind sleep in.

This is not the time for thinking.

It's the time to feel the holiness of things.

A WEEKLY REMINDER

Make eye contact.

Hold my weariness like a glass ball
(gently, gently my darling)
and nestle it
among the soft company
of acceptance and permission.

I am allowed to stumble in the mist.

I am allowed to sway,
to walk clumsily into the dark.

I am allowed to contradict myself,
to stand tall with shaky knees
and lay down
in order to wake up.

AUTUMN'S CALL

We are not the only ones speaking.

The world has much to say
should we entertain the idea
that language extends
far beyond our human tongue.

On Tuesday, the leaves
wouldn't stop chattering to me
about their tales
of transformation,
and how on somedays
the rushing humans
don't even listen
to their yellow swan-songs,
their orange exclamations
and red crescendos
that come just moments
before their great fall
from Branch to Earth.

They worry
of drying unnoticed,
of a brown crunched existence,
of being stepped on
and raked up
without a prior nod
to their autumn splendor.

"We wouldn't mind so much
if you offered us

the attention of your heart
for just a few weeks,
and listened, closely,
to our alluring adieu,"
they told me.

I told them I would try,
before it's too late,
to send their message out
through my poetic medium.

(I hope it works!)

A GROUNDLESS FLOOR

There are moments in life,
when everything you've told yourself
and everything you believe in
fall out from underneath you.
And you sit on a groundless floor
more tender inside
than you ever thought possible,
asking the one question
you know
we can never fully answer,

Why?

No matter what anyone tells you,
don't press yourself
into a perfect package of false compliance.
You are allowed to throw stones at the sky.
To write "fuck" in your journal 74 times
and break into a million little pieces.

You are allowed to ask for help
and wonder, deeply,
about the nature of suffering,
even though you've read a thousand books on the topic
and are supposed to be "the spiritual one."

The truth is beyond what we can see,
and until the veil has truly lifted
sometimes the blindfold
can feel cruel and suffocating.

This is all ok.
Everything
you feel
is ok.
You have not lost your faith.
You are no less of a person.
And when nothing else
soothes you,
apply this balm, slowly,
to your swollen, cracking heart,
and know
you are not alone.

HOLDING BOTH, LIGHTLY

When life becomes heavy,
seek lightness of heart.

When life breaks you apart,
allow a few, selected others
to put you back together.

When life hollows your bones,
infuse laughter into the empty,
dark places.

Don't pretend to be ok.

Don't hide your fragility.

But also, my darling, don't bury your hope.
Or your power.

You will be amazed
how you can hold
both joy and sorrow
elation and deflation
faith and fear
in your most
vulnerable moments.

Your task is
to become
intensely intimate
with the precarious
and strange position

of holding both,
lightly.

And loving.

Always loving.

MARCH UPWARD

You may find yourself
standing
in the middle of a war.

Your choice is to follow
the will of your lower nature
or to use the gateway
of the heart
to walk the subtle path
to your radiant Self.

The choice belongs only to you.

Your true test is only to recognize
when the choice
must be made.

Look for deep inner conflict
and don't rush forward.

Pause intensely.

And realize where you are
and what is at stake.

Then
without impulse
And in deep reflective waters
invoke the angel
of the heart
to guide your way.

You will know of her arrival
when your resplendent courage
is summoned
and falls under the command
of her illustrious gaze.

(March upward).

LULLABIES OF LONGING

Do not let your heart fall asleep.
There is too much riding on its awakening.

When it tires, visit holy places.
When it hurts, look for beauty.
When it overextends, seek solitude.

Don't follow the commotion, crowds and clamor.

You know your holy place.
(Your field, tree, chapel, cushion, cathedral, mat, temple or
ocean wait for you).

Go there often.
Without any agenda.
And let your heart sing
the lullabies of its longing
to keep itself awake.

YOUR MAGIC

In any moment you feel unworthy.

Pause.

Take your magnificent heart
in your hands
and squeeze out
the puddle of nonsense
that has accumulated there
from years of holding back.

You are your own kind of remarkable,
able to make marks upon the world
in unique and astounding ways.

You do not have to remain
as any participatory part
of a conversation that keeps you small.

Anyone who does not understand your magic
simply stumbled in to the wrong show.
Lock eyes with the ones who marvel
and continue on. . .

HOW TO LOVE EVERYTHING

When did you last notice
how alive everything is?
and how desirable?

The world wants to get personal.

The others yearn to matter to you.

When you create space
when you notice
when you feel
when you open your ears
untie your tongue
and place love on your altar of prayer
magic happens.

You are allowed to love (again).

And the problem
will never be how to love
but how to love everything.

Nothing remains dead anymore.

And you.

You come unfathomably alive.

THE WILLOWS OF THE HEART

Surrender your

superiority
delusion
and greed

at the threshold of your awakening.

They have no place here
among the willows of the heart,
whose branches hang low and soft.

Come here often,
and the willows will whisper
a symphony
of medicinal sounds
to calm your critical
and exasperated mind.

A liquid love free-flowing and plenty,
will begin to condense around your throat.
And the words that escape
will carry the nectar and sweetness
of the honeysuckle.

Everything you touch
will simply reflect and affirm
the beauty
of your becoming.

THE HOLY CYCLE OF THINGS

Today was my 12,511th sunset.

And she was spectacular
in her gentle reminder
that on those days,
when your heart
is particularly tender,
you don't wish
for bright, blazing orange
or any plunging,
dramatic departure.

You seek the simple
and soft caress
of peach and violet
as they silently begin
a slow and cautious
descent
to the horizon.

Listen to the silence.
Take a breath,
and remind yourself
that as sure as she is to depart,
she shall return again.

This is the holy cycle of things.

And then cup the empty air
in your aching palms
and lay it as an offering

to the moon
who is not full tonight
and has no need to be.

But still rises
brightly
in her half-ness.

THE RADIANT PATH

Look past the gaze of your fear
to make eye contact
with the dreamer inside of you
that has, for too long,
been neglected.

Then stay put
and make no sudden moves.

Let her awaken
and gather brilliance
under the steady
and unfaltering comfort
of being seen.

Let her know
you're not rushing on again.
That you're done with pleasing others.
That you're done with playing small.

You two must get reacquainted.
Once she trusts you again,
she will have much to say.

But, please,
don't rush the process.

She may not be ready to speak.

Let her find her voice,
in her own time,
but keep your tender gaze steady upon her.
So she knows you are ready
for her alchemy
for her magic that turns pain into purpose,
that places you finally upon
the radiant path
of your becoming.

MAINTENANCE CHECK

Stop treating your fatigue
as a nuisance.

Welcome
the sacred visitor
who has arrived
to take you deep
into yourself,
to fix,
what is no longer working.

DAILY HEART TRAINING

Open when I want to close down.

Stay still when I want to run.

Look when I want to turn away.

Feel when I want to forget.

Be silent when I want to speak.

Forgive when I want to blame.

Look within when I want to project.

Shimmer (yes, shimmer) when I want to stay small.

(Pass it on).

YOUR GALLERY OF DREAMS

Stop obsessively
paving the road.

Speak of soulful things,
and watch for what quickens.

Secretly show someone,
who believes in magic,
the pictures that hang
in your gallery of dreams.
And listen when they tell you
of your loveliness.

Walk slowly into their gaze
and look back
at the marvelous way
your heart gleams
through your eyes
when you speak
of what calls you.

There is nothing more majestic
than witnessing
a life falling open
to the cracking acorn within.

A SIMPLE MORNING RITUAL

Wake up.

Kiss someone.

Drink coffee.

With groggy eyes,
gaze into the magical atmosphere
of your own existence.

Write a love letter to your heart.

And then
live your day
as the reply.

GLUE

Spend time
every day
collecting the pieces
of yourself
that have been broken.

The discarded shards
of inner pain
are the only materials
you need
to build
your stained glass window.

Forgiveness is the glue.

WHAT YOU HAVE COME FOR

Quietly prepare
for your own arrival.

When you wake,
inhale warm rainbow light
and empty the inner trash
with your exhalation.

Lovingly sweep the floor
of your heart
and place a cushion
in front of the altar
next to your pulse.

Bow your head,
and make a simple offering
of love.

Beckon, in a quiet moment,
the deep inner whisper
that knows
why you are here,
and what you have come for.

And then listen.

I beg you
to listen.

WHEN LOST

Seek Holiness

It doesn't matter where
or in what form.
(so stop babbling on about that).

Find something,
anything,
that stirs you,
that fills your heart with an ache,
so gloriously agonizining
that you cannot help
but fall to your knees.

Bow your head.

And remember
in a private, holy moment
the mysteries that move you.

(that is all).

THE SHOULD'S

There's a family
that lives inside of you.

They are called "the Should's."

Welcome them in,
but be extra cautious when they visit.

They are quite convincing, those Should's.

They will find any crack in your consciousness,
to leave their cunning crumbs of mockery.

When you begin to hear their manic debate
—"you should do this. . . you should do that"—
Just smile and take that as your warning.

Keep those crooks close
but only to ensure their eventual demise.

They don't know this,
but when you placed two feet
on your own, unique road
towards inspired, creative living
you already built their grave.

RISE, GODDESS, RISE

Rise, goddess, rise.

Rise, warrior of the winds.
Your sensitive, subtle strength
makes mountains tremble
in reverent awe
and trees reach
down, down, down
in yearning intimacy
with the holy Mother
that lives in your bones.

Rise, woman of the waters.
There is a swelling tide
within you
made not to sit behind a dam
but to rumble and shape the stones
that sit heavy upon the planet's
capacity to feel.

Others may try to keep you small,
but only because they fear
your moon-like magnetism.

Rise, goddess, rise.

It is not the time
to write new legends,
but to bring the ancient,
buried worship back.
To move within circles

and remember, fiercely
that the stars live in your eyes,
and with one blink
you can summon the sun.

Enough of this submissive nonsense.

You were not made
to please
but to dismantle darkness
with your alluring gaze,
to lay siege
upon the fortress
that for, too long,
has kept the wild, feminine heart
chained and captive.

World in your soft, weathered palm,
rise, goddess, rise.

TENDERNESS AND LILIES

Today, the wind captured my panting heart,
and sat me down
in a field of tenderness
and lilies.

"Why am I here?" I asked the wind.
"Among the smiling lilies?"

"Stop trying so hard," the wind whispered.

"Your panting heart cannot keep up
with the ambitions of your mind.
She is tired of chasing dreams,
of feeling not enough,
of rights and wrongs,
and the idea that worth must be earned.

She is choked
from years of self-criticism and angst.

She is short of the Breath
that breathes between breaths
and has temporarily forgotten
the comfort that comes
from the tender knowing
that all is well.

Here, among these lilies,
she is searching for nothing more
than the soft, healing fragrance
of Now."

CHANGING DIRECTION

A packed life has no space
for soul to appear.

You must leave room
for the mysterious winds to blow
between your steps,
for the small moments of wonder
to hold your heart hostage.

You must be willing
to change your direction
when inspiration shrivels,
when the flashing neon sign
in front of your creative joy
reads VACANT.

You must refuse
to disregard what comes to life
when you marvel,
to live a life stripped of stupor.

Stop obsessively chewing
on the contents of your life.

And know when it is time to swallow.

THE UNTARNISHED MOMENT

When Wonderful Things Happen . . .

Stop.

Allow your heart a moment alone
with the spontaneous swelling of joy.

This is the untarnished moment.

This is the moment of pure feeling
that holds no context,
thoughts, judgments, or opinions
of anyone
other than yourself.

This is the quiet moment
of simple and innocent beauty
that demands
absolutely
no
explanation.

When you proclaim wonder
out into the world too quickly,
you miss the sacred minutes
of heart-soaking,
the delicious raw eruption
that belongs
only to you.

A BOUQUET OF POSSIBILITY

Find your way to the dreamer
who lives inside of you.

Make eye contact and smile
but make no sudden moves.

If you approach her
with a bag of fear and skepticism,
she will scurry. And tire.
She will lose her glisten.

But if you offer her a bouquet of possibility
and remain open,
she will etch the most magnificent pictures
onto the walls of your heart
and begin to dismantle (with great glee and pleasure)
the structures of self-doubt
that dampen you.

You are meant to creatively expand
beyond what you can imagine.

She is your guide,
the one who moves
into the mysteries
and (magically) makes things happen.

Whatever you do, don't dismiss her.

Find her and then never (ever) let her go.

POUNDING WITH GRATITUDE

I carry it around
this swollen heart

I wonder often of capacity.

Inner capacity.

If it will simply burst open
and splatter the world
with invisible whispers
that glide on the wind
to soothe the hearts
of my fellow lovers
that are cracked from the same, extended
years
of longing.

I wonder often of saturation.

Inner saturation.

But just when I feel the cup
in my distended chest
cannot hold any more
of your colossal love
the clay softens,
and carefully
another, deeper vessel forms within me.

And I bow astonished
and full before you.

Silent as the soft wind,
and pounding with gratitude.

A WOODEN ALTAR

You came here with a calling.

If you have wandered far
from the lake of your longing,
Stop.
Notice your thirst.
And build a wooden altar.

Wrap your doubt in a silk cloth,
and lay it down
on the weathered planks.

You don't need to exhaust yourself
or feel unworthy any longer.

You don't have to prove anything
or accumulate piles and piles of wisdom.

Your sacred practice
is one of realizing
your soul map
is not something you find,
out of luck,
or excavate from a blistering dig
but something you discover,
out of opening to
inevitability.

A HEALER OF HEARTS

You are a healer.

You have the medicine the world needs
inside of your kind, splendid heart.

You have the magic that we've buried away
inside of your playful imagination.

You have the beauty that we so desperately long for
inside of your whispering soul.

Don't give your power away.
Don't get caught up in helplessness.
Don't seek healing potions in the land outside of yourself.

You are a healer of hearts,
a magician of minds,
and a soul whose radiance in this world
is absolutely necessary.

(Don't dim your dazzle. Period.)

A NEW PARADIGM

Do not for a second
allow yourself to be tamed.

Find your tree, your totem.
And don't tip-toe around anyone.

You are a wild, magnificent mystery.

Go outside.

Revel in awe
at the peculiar glory
of all the creatures around you.
You are one of them.
And they are one of you.
You belong to them.
And they belong to you.

Bury these insane notions
of separation
deep under the ground.
And wait
for a new paradigm
to sprout.

A DEEPER EXISTENCE

Follow your fatigue.

It will lead you on a winding road
towards the truth you've been avoiding.

Busy is not a way to be.

It is a condition that strips you
of meaningful pauses.

It whips you around
in a bowl of self-importance
and pours you out
as a thin layer
upon the surface of your life.

But you seek a much deeper existence.

You seek the substance of silence,
and a slow, simmering awareness.

So please, my darling,
Put down your knife,
Pick up your spoon.

And give your heart the apron.

THE FOAMING TIDE OF ACCEPTANCE

When life hits you in the back of the head. . .

First.
Turn around,
stick your tongue out,
and wave your fist in the air.

Use a few cuss words, if you please.

Stomping is definitely permitted.
And tears are always allowed.

Then.
Have a seat
and close your eyes.

Disperse love throughout your entire body.
And breathe ever so gently
into the pockets of pain.

Hold yourself in a blanket
woven of tender, tender words.
Don't use stops.
Anywhere.
The despair must flow out.
And in.
With the foaming tide of acceptance.

Lay the ever-looming question of "Why?"
down among the shells

that were broken long ago.

And remain
softly on the sand,
ruptured and beautiful,
humming your ache to the wind,
and unfolding wide
to the raw,
unguarded layers of your heart.

A THOUSAND WAYS

There are a thousand ways to come to me.

Raise your hands in exaltation
and I will kiss your palms.

Walk barefoot on sacred ground
and I will soften the earth beneath you.

Bathe in my holy waters
and I will wash over you with love.

Dance freely and with devotion
and I will shower you with grace.

Lay your forehead to the floor and weep
and I will drink your tears.

Use only the most eloquent of words,
speak to me as your neighbor, casual and unpolished,
or come to me in silence.

Sit with your legs crossed or bend your knees to kneel.
Stand up with reverence or lay down beneath my gaze.
Gather to sing my name in unison,
or whisper to me in solitude.

It matters not to me.

What matters is that you feel me within and around you
and you come to me often.

Speak to me of your heart and what moves you.
Tell me the stories of your delight as well as your distress.
Come to me with laughter and desperation,
with a full heart or a broken one

But whatever you do, keep me with you
as the breath that breathes between your breath.

Hold me in the sacred spaces of your heart
as the wind that calls you on.

And let the slow unfolding
of your life's verse
reveal my holy seed
at its center.

THE STARTING POINT

I have planted a flower
of love
within you.

It comes from a seed
that does not grow
with division,
or judgment,
or declaration,
or comparison,
or righteousness.

It is a seed that grows
when you recognize,
with quiet, reverent humility,
that you hold a single flower
in a field of billions
and your roots grow
in the same soil.

When one prevails,
triumph is for all.
When one grows,
all transcend.

I beg of you.
Don't keep each other small.

We've had enough of that.

Your growth depends
upon one another.
And every day you choose
to raise your stalk and block the sun
or bow your head and let me in.

Equality is not the end goal, my beloved ones,
it is the starting point.

FINDING YOUR PATH

Loosen your grip.

Give yourself permission to be imperfect.

Don't seek what others are seeking,
(unless it echoes in your bones).

Spit out whatever you have ingested
about not being enough.

Your realness is delicious.

And you don't need to obsess any longer
about finding your path.

Start simple.

Tie a string
from your heart to your feet
and only walk in the direction
that makes you tick.

SELF LOVE

Acknowledge your gifts.

Notice your beauty.

Don't stay in traps that keep you small.

Shake hands with your critic
and then introduce him to your beloved Self.

There are floods of love within you
that are simply waiting
for the dam of self-judgment to be broken,
for the walls built of your own harsh thoughts
to come crumbling down.

You deserve to know the tenderness
of your own magnificent heart.

Then you will come to know, my beautiful one
that your brilliant capacity to love the world
rests upon how much you love yourself.

STAY HOME

Don't try to speed things up
when they naturally slow down.

Life is not to be lived in a straight line
and time does not only move forward.

Someone is seeking you.

If you rush on
with your own agenda,
the visitor will show up to your door
and find you gone.

Instead, light a candle
and place it in the window of your heart.
Nestle in to a worn pillow of trust
and gaze past the misty glass
into a life that enlarges you.

There will be quiet knock
on your door.
(don't watch the clock).

Your seeker will arrive
when you stop obsessing
about his or her arrival.

And as you revel in wonder,
the two of you will laugh heartily
at how you almost rushed on
and left home.

THE FALLING

Go ahead and fall.

Fall hard.

Your heart is more resilient than your demons
and much more courageous.

Humor them with a conversation,
but smile
knowing that they don't have a chance
going up against love.

Don't give them more power than they deserve.

You were not made for the cliff's edge
but for the plunge far beyond.

When love appears,
it brings a gust of wind
that carries your scars off
to the alchemical well of the gods.

The voices of your demons
will soon hush
under the tones of transformation
and you will begin to see
that love's knife, my darling
is one made for carving.

FLIRT WITH POSSIBILITY

When you feel attacked.

Remember that softness is your strength
and kindness is your shield.

Others will try and tell you
what is not possible.
Just smile and bow.

Then turn immediately around,
blow that crap to the wind,
and wink at the stars.

Go ahead
and flirt with possibility.

Your heart has a wink
that can charm the world
to conspire
with your dreams.

THE SOUL'S PRESCRIPTION

Find the color
that brings you alive.
Place it on your tongue
and swallow
at the first sign
of self doubt.

Drink lots of water
and fall madly in love
with at least one creature.

Boil a cauldron of kindness
and inhale the steam
deeply into your lungs.

Call me in the morning.

INNER PEACE WANTS OUT

You belong to a clan.

You are not destined solely
for individual greatness.

Your greatness is destined
for collective elevation.

Don't you see, my love?

Whatever you cultivate within
is not for you, and you alone.
You must distribute
your inner resources
to a world, parched and thirsty.

If you pay attention,
you will see
with blinding clarity
that

Inner Peace wants out.

YOUR BODY TEMPLE

Your body is wise.

Don't think you know better.
Don't hurry on and shove her aside.

Notice where she hurts.
And where she opens.

Listen carefully to the story of her wounds,
and by all means, whatever you do,
don't keep telling her lies.

She is your doorway in.
And your doorway out.

She is a temple. A church pew.
A patch of dark, beautiful earth.

She is a merchant of the Mysteries.

Trade with belittling commands,
and she will not abide.

But appear with sacks of loving whispers,
and she will reveal the pure magic
of your mortal existence.

WHAT INTERESTS ME

I am interested in simple beauty.

I am interested in the way the pupils of the heart
dilate from a single flash of sweetness.

I am interested in how you move into what scares you,
how you sketch your dreams upon the sands of your soul,
and how you tell your legend.

I am interested in how you cradle others,
how you offer the soft, cushion of your compassion to the
world.

I am interested in how the moonlight falls upon your face,
and whether or not you soften into the folds of the sunlight
at dawn.

And I am interested, my darling, in how you want us all to
know you,
in whether or not you will leave crumbs of kindness
for the world to follow home when lost.

A HOLY REUNION

I fell asleep and when I awoke,
I tip-toed to the window
so not to wake the sleeping snow.

I wanted to inquire of her arrival,
etch the stories that have passed
since we last conversed,
scold her for being absent and withdrawn. . .
but thought
I should not disturb the silent lullaby
she was already humming in my heart.

She has seduced time with her alluring caress
and lays like a blanket upon my eyes
and the road beneath them.

She has turned the relevance
of my wandering mind into vapor.

And left me perched,
quietly,
upon this single moment
of our holy reunion.

FOLLOWING THE QUESTION

What is peace?

My love, it is not
about answering that question,
but following it.

There are holy crumbs for you to trace
to a pond deep within.

This pond is glistening blue
and still
among the frenetic winds
of time and change.

The waters are pure
and unpolluted
and as you dip
even the tip of your finger
into its warmth,
it will spread up your arms
and to your heart,
until everything within and around you,
while physically the same,
is now glowing
and nestled
perfectly into place.

THE MUSIC OF CONNECTNESS

Holy recognition is rare.

When it happens,
you will find yourself
drop
into the deep, warm sponge
at the center of your heart.

An eye will emerge
that sees beyond
the physical forms
and cannot blink
from the tender beauty
of the soul before you

The only chord
the fibers of your being play
is "yes."

And the holy music
of our connectedness
caresses the inner folds
of your ear
until all sounds
howl of oneness.

A BOW AND AN OFFERING

Watch yourself carefully.

Notice what seeds you plant
and the way your eyes
catch the light in your kindness.

Take gentle note of your stumbling
but shine also your gaze
upon your marvelously beautiful stride.

Allow graciousness to flush your cheeks.

Make strangers blush
with your recognition
of their undeniable loveliness.

Upon a sacred encounter,
follow the cobbled road
of compassion
to the doorway
of their heart

Knock ever so gently.
And whisper of holiness.

When the door opens,
always enter
with a bow
and an offering.

THE WATERY GAZE

Find a moment to be still.

And in that moment, allow an unfolding - wide, tender and striking.

I have long awaited an allowance to place my palm.

I have long awaited a vulnerability that softens under my watery gaze

and does not collapse with my touch.

Unfold the petals and you will see.

The receptive soil of your heart
is the precious land
upon which
I buried your purpose

Your task now, my love,
is simply
to open to the rain.

THE SULTAN'S GOLD

Don't wait any longer.

You must wring out your saturated heart.

Empty the contents, with urgent haste,
and lay them out before you.

Look upon them with a gaze,
fixed and discerning.

Don't you see?

Anger chokes the tenderness from your eyes.

Resentment festers among the mildew of your past

And fear has left you torn and abandoned.

Wring them out, and leave them
upon the softened soil.

Pick up only what can be wrapped
in the holy silk of your heart.

And carry that as your currency
to trade in this world of merchants.

The jewels of love
are infinitely more precious
than even the Sultan's gold.

YOUR LIFE IS LARGE

When the tender ache descends,
you will know.

You are being summoned.

I beg of you not to numb the pain
or ice the swelling.

You will find yourself among a glistening world,
searching for ancient brass.

Stay low.
Below the cacophony that tries to dissuade you.

Drink of the empty cup,
until radiant silence is smeared
on your gorgeous face.
And you finally recognize your eyes.

Your life is large. Your being masterful.
And nothing but you
may alter the divinity
that has begun its reveal.

A HEART-CENTERED CONSTITUTION

Don't drink the poison.

When the cup is handed to you,
smile,
nod your head,
and put it down.

The time has come
to live beyond the literal.

To remember the fairy folk
and invisible ones
who sing on mossy ground
and slide down weathered bark.

To love again the rooted trees,
and wing-ed ones.

There is a new heart-centered constitution.

If you sign,
even the sound of trickling water
can send you into a trance.

This is when
the eyes of the heart
begin to blink open
to a world
terribly euphoric
in her loveliness.

THE SEARCH FOR SPACE

Listen deeply.

There is a stifled voice
underneath the clutter
that needs spaciousness
to find the clarity of its tone.

Don't evoke will or aggression
in an attempt to plow
hurriedly towards it
but softly wait
and send whispers of love
to entice its emergence
from beneath the fog.

This is a sacred meeting
that begs your full capacity
of tenderness and warmth
and will return it
a thousand times over
should you choose
to let go.

OWNING IT

You.
You are all kinds of sexy
when you stop wishing to be anyone
except the dripping beauty that you are.

You are all kinds of stunning
when you soften the rigid lines
of your body and mind,
and welcome the washing tides
of vulnerability.

Don't sell your truth
to the devious merchants of self-doubt.

Don't give away your power
to the thieves of insecurity.

Don't tell yourself anymore lies.
And please, my wild darling,
don't believe the lies
that have been told to you.

Begin to shatter
the false notions
that keep you small
and refuse to meet the world
in anything less
than your fierce, vast gorgeousness.

You were made to unleash
your own inner beauty.

And absolutely nothing
is more breathtaking
than your own divinity
in revelation.

YOUR OWN ARRIVAL

Each day, carve a moment
to reflect,
to find the vast, blue stillness
within you.

Don't trip on the obstacles.

There is a part of you
that knows the way.

Just nod and follow.

Each time you return here,
you will receive a radiant
and warm welcome.

You've been awaiting
your own arrival,
quietly preparing
with attentiveness and love.

There is no formal invitation.

So stop waiting at the shore,
for your grand departure,
and simply walk back inside.

INNER BEAUTY

Your imperfection
makes you real.

There is little beauty
that extends beyond
a wise and weathered heart,
a heart that chooses to feel
in order to honor all that it has lost,
a heart that continues to tick
in order to revere the tragedies it has overcome,
a heart that bows
before the mysteries that melt us
and has learned the ancient alchemy
of transforming pain
into power and purpose.

THE UNTANGLING

When you find yourself conflicted,
don't rush, my darling.

Find some time alone
to disentangle your voice
from the voice of others within you.

Take shelter
under the sacred roof of silence.

Slowly unwind from the ways
you have been conditioned.
And wait for a clear impulse to appear.

There is no wrong path.

What matters is how you make the path you choose the right one.

And understand the immense power
you hold within
to (re)direct the tides
of your Holy Emergence.

WILD VINES

Take some time away
from the clutches of the city.

There is an untamed wind
that calls you
and has carved a crevice
in the dark soil
for you to find
your sense of wild expanse,
again.

This connection of yours
to Earth
is nothing short of necessary.

She has been asking for you.

And after she takes you in for some time
you will emerge
with lush, shimmering eyes
and vines of wonder
growing, wildly, from your heart.

A SACRED MARRIAGE

On this day
I invited you to join
the sacred prayer of my life.

And you entered
with such remarkable graciousness
that you managed
to walk within me
without disturbing my worship.

In fact, you came
so gently and reverently
into the secret cove
where I converse with God
that somehow
without any jolt or interruption
you have so effortlessly joined
and radically deepened
my most holy conversation.

A SOFT, LOVING MOMENT

There is a layer
of hopes, fears, and attachments
that we stack upon
the essence of our experience.

Beloved one, try and allow yourself
in a soft, loving moment
to feel what you feel,
to hear what you hear,
to think what you think
without rushing to judge
or determine
or label
or suppress
or attach.

There is a vast blue ocean
below the surface waves.

And it whispers in tides
that wash over your mind
with healing waters of
simple, pure acceptance,
softhearted spaciousness
and gentle, gentle love.

TURNING WITHIN

Heart-centered being,
whatever you do,
don't continue to give
when you are empty.

Know your boundaries.

Move into a soft corner
of your heart
and give yourself permission
to stop.
To say no.

Ask for what you need,
but understand
that there is a Source within you
that already knows.

All you have to do
is turn towards it.

A HAZY MIRAGE OF WONDER

When the world around you
looks grey,
bring brightness to your eyes.

Soften your gaze
so the harsh lines
blur
into a hazy mirage of wonder.

Lead with your vulnerability
and speak to random hearts
with the wide, open field
of your spirit.

We are all listening.

And the ears of the heart

never tire

of hearing

the glorious

whistles

of the soul.

BOUYANCY

When you find yourself in turbulent waters
tie a rope to your center
and loosen your hold.

Your tight grip
only fastens to fear
and chokes your flexibility.

Trust the buoyancy of your heart.

It knows these waves
and the elasticity it takes
to weather the storm.

In your moment of distress
don't frantically stiffen
but invoke the deep malleability
that only the holy wisdom
of the heart
may beckon.

There is no other rescue
in this moment, my darling
than this.

Until the storm subsides.

TENDING A SACRED OASIS

It is softness
that will unlock your lips.

The corners raise
when the heart valve releases.

A steam of tenderness
rises up
to possess you.

In this possession,
your breath infuses the world
with a holy sweetness
and your words
pollinate
the invisible, wild flowers
of love
until an entire garden
sprouts from your soul.

Don't you see?
You were born to tend
this sacred oasis.

You hold fields and fields
of divine potential
within you.

And we are long awaiting
the diffusion
of your particular fragrance.

THE ANGEL OF THE HEART

Your heart
is a being of love.

Approach her gently
and her fires of devotion
will rise like holy lava.

Project sweetness
and she will guide you
to the gateway
of higher consciousness.

This angel holds the key,
which will unlock
deep tides of oneness
with all sentient beings.

Without her,
doors to the infinite
are heavy and cumbersome.

But a strong gust
of her tender breath
blows the petals
of your divine heart
wide, wide open.

We belong
to a system of love,
my fellow seekers.
And thus cannot escape

the allure and longing
of the Heart.

UNDERNEATH THE VEIL

There is no magic formula except this:

Find what you feel is Holy and follow it.

Follow it with every breath.
Let every inhale
and every exhale
pull you
further
into its magnificence.

This pursuit is only yours.

Persuasion comes from the lips
of your heart,
and your heart alone.

From here forward, my love,
every doubting voice
will dissolve
into the beauty
you are becoming.

And silence
will fall upon the loud voice
that for too long
has kept you veiled.

A NOTE FOR THE ACHING HEART

Aching ones, be gentle with yourself.
The heart is a vessel of alchemy.
Place your pain within its chamber,
and whatever you do
don't close the lid.

The steam must escape.

Breathe tender breaths.
Slowly.
Infused with holiness.

Trust that the angel of love
within you
holds a glowing ember
whose flame cannot be extinguished.

Invite the warmth into the painful, aching places
and stay still for a while.

You are whole.
You are healing.
You are divinely resilient.
And this too shall pass.

A HOLY PRISM

Maybe someone,
some time ago
made you feel small, peculiar, sensitive,
strange or not good enough.

Maybe someone,
some time ago
made you feel misunderstood, disregarded,
unimportant, outcast or invisible.

Maybe you've moved on,
grown up,
persevered.

And yet those voices
still remain like seeds
that sprout when the rains
of self-doubt appear.

Come here, my darling.
And let me tell you
(until your ears flop over with fatigue)
how undeniably lovely you are,
how the world has called in
the peculiar, pulsing hearts (like yours)
to break down the thick walls o
of estrangement.

Maybe you cannot see it,
but when I look at your heart,
it is not flat or misshapen

or too open or over-used.

It is a holy prism.

When light enters you,
it scatters as glorious colors
upon the gray world
of complacency.

No one can tell you
to live in a white world anymore.

You already started reflecting the new world.
Long, long ago.
(Keep doing your thing, beautiful)

RECOGNIZE YOUR DIVINITY

Every day get in touch with something holy.
The heart needs stirring to stay awake.

You don't have to follow anyone, anywhere.
Soul does not hand out prescriptions.

Light a candle before the angel
that resides within you.
And wait for the whispers of love.

Sacredness is everywhere.

Promise yourself
that busyness
will not become your god
and unworthiness
will never be your mantra.

You are a wild, magnificent mystery.

And your divinity comes alive
with the stoking breath
of recognition.

WILLING TO FLOW

Try to be open.
Less rigid.

Try to be curious.
Less decisive.

Try to be fluid.
Less stagnant.

Try to be flexible.
Less stubborn.

Try to be kind.
Less critical.

When I see you are willing to flow,
I will take you straight
to the ocean.

WOMAN OF THE WILD

Woman of the wild,
be still.
Feel the river in your veins
and take the warmth of the sun
far under your skin.

Close your eyes
until the exhaustive and expecting world
disappears
and you finally find your
full, untamed
exhalation.

You were not made
with pleasing in mind.

What pleases your mind,
wild one,
is the feeling in your bones
of from what (and whom) you are made.

When you feel this,
no storm can rage strong enough
to scare you.
No amount of temptation
can bind you.
And a roaring, focused strength
swells from the peaceful lake
deep inside of your heart

Your mantra today:

I am from Gaia.
I am from Gaia.
I am from Gaia.
And I dare you to try to dissuade me
from walking my Truth
and awakening my Power.

A PROMISE TO MYSELF

When I want to argue,
Begin a conversation
(And remember to listen)

When I want to bury my feelings,
Find a kind way to express them.
(And remember to listen)

When I worry about conflict,
Prioritize growth and evolution.
(And remember to listen)

When I want to turn away,
Walk in the direction of my distress.
(And remember to listen)

When I want to react,
Pause. And get quiet. Really quiet.
(And remember to listen)

The ear
is the organ of receiving
oneself
and all of those around us.

ENOUGH

As a heart-centered being,
your challenge is to know
when to shut the door
on those who drain or poison you.

To rise up and say,
"This person has already taken up
too much of my time,
my life, my energy
and my holy heart space."

Lock your need to please away
in a vault
and put your hands on your heart
in strength and compassion.

Then, without hesitation,
escort them out of your temple
with clarity, conviction and love.

This is holy work.
You
and only you
have to create the conditions
and space you need
for your sacred expansion.

YOUR NAKED HEART

When your eyes are tired
don't stare into the blinding light.

In order to dilate the pupils of your heart
close them gently and rest
in the darkness of this mystery.

This Life
does not ask your permission
or beg your friendship.

It does not place suffering quietly
on the ground at your feet.

This Life
will test your resilience
demand your pliability
and will not ask politely
before it peels away
the tough outer skin
you have formed
around your heart.

But your naked heart, my love
is hauntingly beautiful.

It is made of divine fibers
whose strength and courage
are soft and tender, and yet
far surpass our mortal toughness.

Your naked heart
is the only one
who can lead you
to the holy and miraculous river
of surrender.

THE YELLOW BOAT

When the clouds move in,
find a yellow boat
to take your tangled hair
and untamed heart
out to the horizon.

To the place where
rough seas are not feared.

The place where the shifting winds
sing about the consistency
of change.

Sure as the clouds move in,
they shall move out.

Sure as the sun descends,
it shall rise soon after.

Sure as the heart breaks,
it shall be glued back together.

Sure as the soul leaves,
it shall return again.

Sure as your mind questions,
it shall rest
(finally)
in the answers.

When you ache,
don't focus on the clouds.

Find your yellow boat,
the state of heart
that will (somehow) transport you
to the wise one
who holds the rope
and the anchor.

It was already dropped
long ago.

You cannot venture out alone too far.

INNOCENCE

I'm not sure we ever know
where it goes.

Those marble eyes
polished by the purity
of untarnished joy
and wonder.

That buoyant heart
that prances lightly
upon the atmosphere,
unafraid to kiss a stranger
or the wide, open sky
with a smile
so unabashedly cheery.

I like to think
there is an inner shrine
with invisible guardians
built around a simple
and ever-glowing curiosity.

We never lost it.

We just forgot how to listen.

The winding road
kidnapped our eager glee.

But delight can never
be caged for long.

Deep within,
we still are
(and always will be)
exuberantly
giggling.

A TENDER BALANCE OF EFFORT AND SURRENDER

There is great unrealized potential within you.

New stories must be written,
as the old pages of self doubt decay.

Don't rummage through the garbage.

Simply allow evolution to unfold
through a tender balance of effort and surrender.

You are not meant for the flat lands.

The mountains of self discovery are calling.
And will remind you of your internal fortitude when you
weaken.

The rivers of mastery beckon.
And will whisper of fluidity and purification when you
harden.

It is up to you when you will join the sacred tribe,
Dedicated to the great inner journey.
Home.

KARMA

If you want others
to sprinkle stardust
on your success
then
sprinkle stardust
on the success
of others.

If you don't want envy
puked on your masterpiece
then
don't puke envy
on the masterpiece
of others.

Overlapping radiance
is what makes the whole world
glow.

SETTING GOALS

You don't have to apply pressure.

To choose one direction.
Or another.

To write down one resolution.
Or another.

You may give your heart room to breathe,
to move freely amidst your dreams.

You may allow her space
to run among the long blades of grass,
to wander in your ever-changing aspirations,
leaving her fingerprints on the dandelion weeds.
Not sure what to pull yet
or what to plant.

You may provide her
a small morsel of time
to absorb the sacred reality
that you have already aspired much,
accomplished much, dreamt much, helped much,
suffered much, transformed much, and loved much.

That your life
has been a long process
of alignment.

Bringing your heart closer
and ever closer

to your own divine pulse.

Something pulls you
like a magnet
into a holy resonance.

One resolution
perhaps
could be
to let yourself be pulled.

You no longer have to fear
your own resistance.

Release the self applied tension
and
let yourself
be pulled.

CARE FOR THE DISCARDED

Some parts of you lay nascent and bare.

Waiting.

It takes courage to care for the discarded,
to tend to the heap of broken glass,
the fragile voices, the barely opened seeds.

Fall, my darling, into the soft soil within you,
and begin to collect the pieces of your potential.

Don't be selective and grab only at what sparkles.

Take your time to till the land
of your majestic vulnerability.

Whisper to the gray and undeveloped parts of your psyche.
Tell them of your patience.

Pull the weeds, kiss them,
and place them, lovingly, aside.

Walk barefoot
and invite the critters to come along.

This journey, as gardener, my beloved friend,
is as much about the dirt,
as it is about the sun,
as much about the roots,
as it is about the blossoms.
It is, you must realise,

as much about care,
as it is about cultivation.

TO BE TERRIBLY IN LOVE WITH THE WORLD

If there is a longing, look to it.
Place it on your tongue.

But do not swallow.

Hold it just long enough
to extract its essence,
to taste its origin.

This is the elixir
that will return all of the sacred minerals
that have been stripped away from you.

This is the potion
that with one drop will
cast a spell upon your trodden heart
and restore your marvel.

This is the tonic
that has been brewed
to make you finally accept
that you are terribly in love with this world

And the world is terribly in love with you.

ABOUT THE AUTHOR

Deborah Anne Quibell's creative path began as a child when she started writing poetry around the age of five. She fell in love with the mystics in her teens, and began a life of insatiable spiritual inquiry, living on four of the seven continents.

She has taught healing and meditation for over 14 years, and studied under the personal guidance of Master Choa Kok Sui, the founder of modern Pranic Healing and Arhatic Yoga. She holds a PhD in Depth Psychology with emphasis in Jungian and Archetypal Studies.

She is the co-author of *Deep Creativity: Seven Ways to Spark Your Creative Spirit,* released by Shambhala Publications in March 2019. She has also engaged with some of the top online international publications. She is a passionate creative, and believes in breathing grounded knowledge from scholarly pursuits into the fields of mysticism and spirituality, while staying accessible to a wide audience through humor, heart, poetics, and grace. She is a senior instructor for the Institute for Inner Studies and teaches pranic healing, yoga, and meditation throughout Europe and the United States.

She now lives in Rome, Italy with her husband and son, and is constantly searching for magic and meaning amidst the beautiful mess of modern day life.

Made in the USA
Coppell, TX
08 December 2021

67621761R00075